Breathless Bridal Presents:

Before You Say Yes!

A Brides' Guide to Selecting the Perfect Dress

Michel Bailey

Copyright Michel Bailey 2019

All rights reserved. No part of this book may be reproduced or used in any manner without written permission of the copyright owner except for the use of quotations in a book review. For more information, Address: P.O. Box 548

Greenbrier TN. 37073

FIRST EDITION

www.breathlessbridal.com

ISBN:978-1-7330912-0-6 (paperback)

978-1-7330912-1-3 (ebook)

Dedications

I want to dedicate this book to my family.

To my mom, Dolores Counts, who has supported and loved me my entire life! She is not only my sweet mom, she is a wonderful friend! She was the first to instill in me the love of sewing and She has taught me so much! She set a course for her future generations to follow, and we certainly have! Thank you Mom and I love you!

To my four beautiful daughters: Felicity, Jesslyn, Stephanie, and Brianna. You have all grown into beautiful young women. I couldn't live without your love and support. I am so proud of all of you!

And especially to the love of my life; Jurgen. His constant love, tireless support, and encouragement have gotten me through life with courage and grace. I never would have made it without him! He is my heart and soul! To honor him was the reason I wore the greatest dress I could get my hands on! I love you Darling!

Acknowledgements

A big THANK YOU to the beautiful couples who were kind enough to share their photos with me: To Joel and Joanna Zimmerle for theirs photos for the front cover, exquisite!

A special thank you to the Zimmerle photographer Shots by Cheyenne, Cheyenne Goodman for allowing me to use her gorgeous work.

I want to give a very big thank you to Seth and Alyssa Choate for the veil photo in Chapter 10, Absolutely Stunning!

A special Thank you to the Choate photographer, Mandy Chadwick for allowing me to use her fantastic work. Contact information for these photographers can be found in my resource section.

Thank you to my daughter Jesslyn Carver who walked me through this process and put up with me for this past year getting this together. Your artistic sketches, photography and editing are priceless!

A big thank you goes to my daughter Brianna for your textile knowledge and couture expertise! You have tremendous talent and will go far!

Thank you to my husband Jurgen, for his undying support and for taking care of things while I was glued to the computer. I couldn't do it without you!

Contents

Introduction	7
Chapter 1: Selecting the Right Dress for You.	11
Chapter 2: A Dress for Every Body	19
Chapter 3: The Gown	31
Chapter 4: Undergarments and Closures	47
Chapter 5: Fabrics	51
Chapter 6: Where to Buy	67
Chapter 7: Alterations	77
Chapter 8: Destination and Themed Weddings	91
Chapter 9: Second Brides	97
Chapter 10: To Veil, Or Not To Veil?	99
Chapter 11: Corset, Buttons and Bustles, "Oh My!"	105
Conclusion	124
Resources	125
About the Author	126

Introduction

He asked and you said "Yes." Oh Happy Day! Now you must say yes again, "Yes" to a *Dress!* Selecting a bridal gown is one of the most exciting times in a bride's life! Many girls dream of their gown their entire lives; others never give it a second thought until the question is popped and the reality of the decision descends. What will you wear? For some it is a happy decision, for others a stressful uncomfortable time.

I want to take the stress out of the dress! Whether you've sketched your dream gown all over your high school notebooks, or hate the idea of wearing a dress, this book is for you!

My goal is to use my 40 years of seamstress experience and help you select the gown that compliments your body and brings out that bridal glow!

The bride is the star of the show! Her first appearance at the back of the venue is the moment many girls dream of. This is the stuff that makes moms and dads tear up, along with every tenderhearted friend or loved one. To achieve this heart stopping moment, the dress has to be special, unique to you, awe inspiring, and breathless!

Let me walk you through the steps of selecting the perfect gown to compliment you.

First, I'll cover body shapes and the importance of balancing the shape when considering gowns. I'll talk about where to find this gown to ensure you find quality. I'll cover how the gown is built and what to wear underneath it. I'll explain why alterations are important and what to expect when you go in for your fitting. In chapter eleven, I have tips for mothers-of-the-brides and maids-of-honor on how to lace a corset back, and bustle up the train. Although it may be helpful to read this book from cover to cover, I'm writing it so that you can skip to the chapters as you need them.

Congratulations on your future marriage and we here at Breathless Bridal wish you all the best!

Chapter 1

Selecting the Right dress for you!

On July 29th of 1981 I got out of bed in the wee hours of the morning, full of excitement, to witness the Royal Wedding between Lady Diana Spencer and Prince Charles. Certainly one of the hottest topics in anticipation of the day was, "What will she wear?" Well let me tell you, she did not disappoint! Everyone has seen her gown by now. I remember being awe struck as she reached the top of the stairs going into the church and her train was touching the ground below.

The gown was designed by David and Elizabeth Emanuel who stated, "A dress that had to be something; that was going to go down in history, but also something that Diana loved;" "Suitably dramatic in order to make an impression."(en.wikipedia.org/wiki/wedding_dress_of_lady_Diana_Spencer

What a dress! She had a 25 ft. train with 10,000 pearls. Her gown was ivory silk taffeta and lace, with a fitted, boned bodice, curved neckline, and a detailed finish. Her sleeves were in true 80's fashion, large and bulbous. It was a jaw-dropping sight, certainly worth awakening in the early hours.

Kate Middleton, who married Diana's oldest son, Prince William wore a less lavish gown but elegant nonetheless. Her gown was designed by Sara Burton of Alexander McQueen. "Miss Middleton wished for her dress to combine tradition and modernity with the artistic vision that characterizes Alexander McQueen's work. " The Palace stated. (8 suprising things you might not know about Kate Middleton's wedding dress by Maggie Maloney May 15, 2018)

Kate's train was considerably shorter than Diana's, trailing a mere 9 feet in length. (Maloney, 2018)

Unlike Diana, Kate's gown was more Victorian inspired as it had a corseted waist and padded slightly below the mid-section. (Maloney, 2018)

The lace was handmade by the Royal School of Needlework, based at Hampton Court Palace, using a technique from Ireland from the 1820's called carrickmacross lace making. The bodice, skirt, and underskirt trim was created out of English and French Chantilly lace. (Maloney, 2018)

Michel Bailey

A more recent royal wedding was that of Meghan Markle to Prince Harry, younger brother to Prince William. Meghan chose a minimal elegance design by Givenchy designer Clare Waight Keller. Her simple elegance gown was made of double bonded silk and featured a boat neck neckline with ¾ length sleeves. Her veil provided the train at 16. 5 feet in length with hand embroidery gracing the edges.
(How Meghan Markle's Wedding Dress Compared to Kate Middleton's, By Lauren Alexis Fisher, May 19, 2018)

All three gowns are fit for a princess and yet very different. Each one expresses the unique personality of the bride who wore it. Is there a right or wrong gown? Certainly not! It all depends on the lady it adorns.

The selection of styles and fabric choices can be overwhelming. It's not always easy to know what style and fabric will be suited for your nuptials and more importantly your personality! Will you be having an outdoors wedding? Barn weddings are very popular as of this writing. Perhaps a destination or a church wedding is more your style. Each choice of venue carries its own style of events.

Generally, selecting the venue should come first in wedding preparations, and gown selection should be right behind it. It's important to begin as early as possible, because the time it takes an ordered gown to arrive seems to be growing. If you are open to purchasing a gown that was used as a sample in a dress shop or a used gown for sale by consignment, then it isn't necessary to order a gown. However, if you want a full choice in selection in both style and fabric, early is always better!

How early? Shopping a year in advance of the wedding is a great idea. Your local boutique can give you an estimate on the amount of time you can expect for your gown to arrive.

Don't forget to allow time for alterations. Almost every bride will require some alterations to her gown once it arrives. I have met perhaps two brides that found a dress to fit perfectly including the hem. Honestly, they may have bought their gowns second hand and the dress had already been altered. We will go into alterations in a later chapter.

So your first task is to talk with your partner and decide where you want to have this lifetime experience. Immediately after that decision is made, it's time to think about getting that dress!

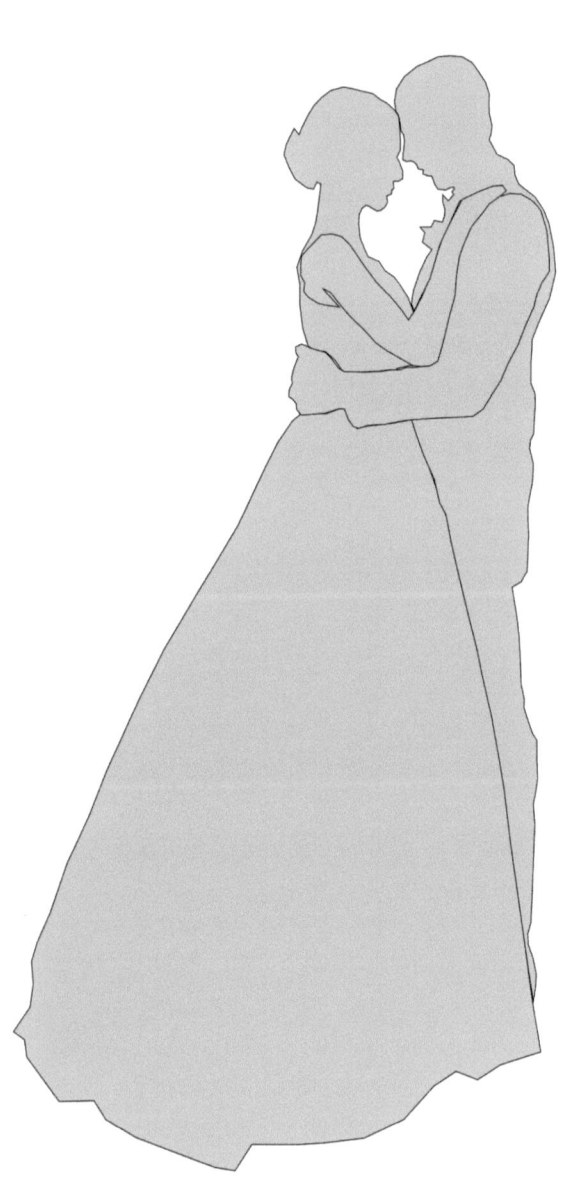

Chapter 2

A Dress for Every Body!

What looks good on you? Do you even know? What looks good on your sister or best friend may not look as good on you! Everybody is different, but everyone can look their best if they know how to select styles that complement their unique figure, skin tone and personality.

In this chapter I will talk about body types as it applies particularly to the wedding dress. There are several different silhouettes in wedding gown styles and they all compliment and accentuate different features of the body. Select the wrong style for you and you just accentuated a feature you may rather minimize.

Before I get started, let me say that we are all different and perfect just as we are! There is no right shape or right size. The fashion industry has set a standard for proportions as a starting point for fitting purposes. No one should feel shamed or embarrassed about their dress size number or proportions. Few people ever fit the standard exactly. But they had to start somewhere; so size charts are nothing more than a starting point for finding your perfect dress.

I also want to state that what style of gown you select is a personal decision. There really are no "right or wrongs" when it comes to bridal gowns. When you look in the mirror, you know if you like what you see. I am merely trying to help take some of the guess work out for you. So you can make some of these decisions on purpose instead of stumbling through them. (www.craftsy.com, Knit to Flatter with Amy Herzog)

There are basically 4 body silhouettes to be aware of:

Large Bust Silhouette: Shoulders/Bust area appears wider than hips and thigh leg area.

Large Hip Silhouette: Hips and thigh area appears wider than shoulder and bust area.

Proportioned Silhouette: Shoulder/Bust area and hip/thigh area share the same measurment with a smaller waist measurement in between (7 or more inches).

Straight Silhouette: Measurements between the bust, hip and waist are close to the same with perhaps only an inch or so difference.

In a nut shell it's all about balance! You want to balance the bust with the hips and bring them into proportion to each other. If you are big-busted, you may want to add to your hip area and minimize your bust area by not selecting gowns that bring attention to the bust. (Herzog, 2013)

Other features of body shape that you may want to keep in mind are having a short-waist, or long-waist. Do you have a straight torso (straight silhouette) or a curved torso (proportioned silhouette)?

There are a lot of little tricks to achieve these goals. My bet is you're practicing them already and not even aware of it. Hopefully, this chapter will help you determine what silhouette you feel most comfortable with and save you agonizing time in the dressing room.

Large Bust Silhouette

If you have a large bust area, you may want to draw attention toward your hips while minimizing the bust with 3/4 or long sleeves.

Suggested Dress Silhouette:

Mermaid, Trumpet, A-line, Shealth.

Small Bust/larger hip Silhouette

If you are small busted with broader hips, you may want to accent the bust area with a short or cap sleeve. (Herzog, 2013)

Suggested Dress Silhouettes: A-line, Ballgown, Empire waist, Short Sleeves.

Proportioned Silhouette

If you have a proportioned silhouette, then ideally you will want to maintain that look. Proportioned silhouettes can wear most any style with little changes.

Suggested Dress Silhouettes: Mermaid, Trumpet, A-line, Shealth, Ballgown.

Straight Silhouette

If you have a straight Silhouette you will want to create definition between the Bust, hip and waist area. This can be acheived by using several features. Short sleeves will make the bust appear larger and a dropped waist may give the waist line more definition.

Suggested Dress Silhouettes: Shealth, A-line, Empire waist, ballgown with droppped waist.

Finding Your Particular Shape

Get your measurements before you begin gown shopping. This can be done at home or hopefully the shop you visit will have someone there who knows how to properly measure.

Take the bust measurement

To get your bust measurement, place the measuring tape around the fullest part of the bust and have the tape gently meet in the middle. You do not want a tight measurement or one that has space between the body and the tape. The tape should lie comfortably against the body.

Take your waist measurement

This is achieved by wrapping the measuring tape around the torso at the most narrow part of the waist just below the rib cage. These days we wear our jeans resting on top of our hips and we have come to believe that that is the waist. Our true waist is just below the ribs. Pull the tape comfortably around the body, meeting with no gap and not too tight. If the tape is pulled to tightly, you'll get a false measurement.

Take your hip measurement

Again, wrap the tape around the fullest part of the hip usually at the center of the buttocks, meeting comfortably, not too tight. Sometimes the upper thigh area is wider than the hips, if that is the case take a measurement of both. This may or may not be an issue, depending on the dress you select.

Out of these three numbers, the largest body part will determine the size gown you will need to purchase with the exception of perhaps the ball gown. The ball gown is usually gathered at the waist and flows out at the hips. Therefore, the size required for a ball gown may be determined by the bust or waist measurement and not the hips even if the hips are larger than the bust.

The cut of the dress will make this determination. Also keep in mind that each designer will have their own size chart so the size may vary between designers.

For example if the hips have the highest measurement and pushes the gown purchase into a larger size, then most likely the bust and waist, will have to be taken in during alterations. It's always better to have the gown slightly larger than too small!

TIP: *Make sure your sales girl checks the size chart of the designer you have selected, before ordering your dress. No time for mistakes when ordering!*

Chapter 3

The Gown

Silhouettes

Bridal gowns come in several silhouettes and these silhouettes can be used to balance your body shape for the most attractive results. When paired with different waistlines, sleeves and necklines, almost every silhouette can be tailored to compliment any bride.

Here are the silhouettes:

A-Line *Ballgown*

Trumpet

Shealth

Fit and Flare

Mermaid

Waistlines

A variety of waistlines are available in combination with these silhouettes to make every silhouette complimentary to any figure.

Here are those waistlines:

Basque

Dropped

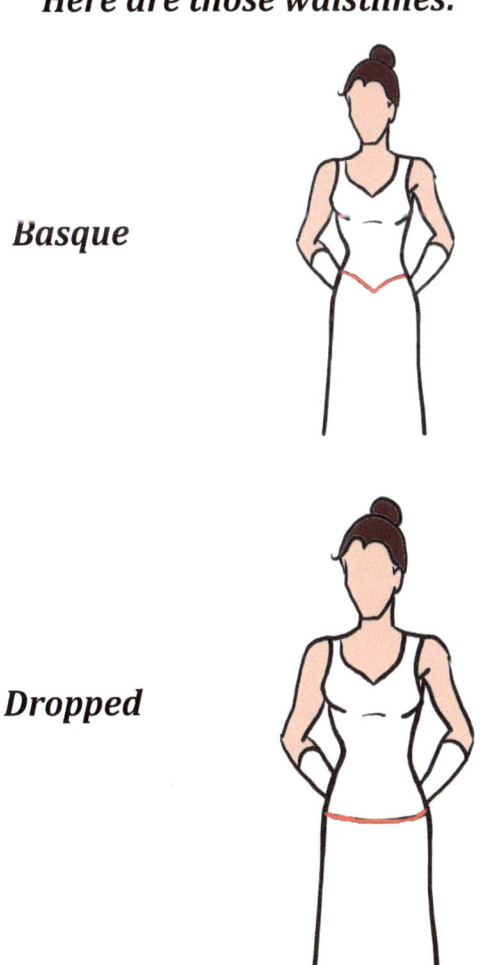

Before You say "YES"

Natural

Princess

Empire

If you are short and, perhaps, have a short waist, a ball gown with a natural waist line may make you appear even shorter. A bride can remedy this, if she wants to wear a ball gown, by selecting one with a dropped waist. The dropped waist gives the appearance of a longer torso and lengthens the body.

Fit and Flare and Trumpet silhouettes are very popular at this writing. A curvy figure can easily enjoy the sleek appearance of a fit and flare. A petite bride with a straight figure may think a fit and flare is just not for her. However there are things she can do to make the straight figure appear curvier. A fit and flare with cap sleeves or short sleeves will bring attention to the bust area and make it look bigger which will help in developing that curvy look for the straight figure. Bra cups can also be sewn into the gown to enhance the bust line for a fuller appearance.

A-line gowns are very forgiving for the Larger-hip silhouette bride. The fitted extended bodice and gentle transition into the full skirt minimizes the hip area. Cap sleeves can again be added to the A-line gown for the larger-hip silhouette bride to balance her figure and give her the look she wants. The straight silhouette dress can also be worn by any body shape if proper attention is given to the waistline.

Again a dropped waist or Basque waistline will be much more attractive for a short-waisted bride and balance will have to be taken into consideration for the overall appearance.

A straight silhouette gown with empire waist is attractive on a proportioned figure or a small busted figure. The empire waist naturally gives the appearance of a larger bust.

A natural waistline breaks just below the rib cage and can give the appearance of added pounds to a figure, especially the straight sihouette bride. Balance will need to be maintained between the bust and the hips.

A princess waistline is very slimming as it has long seams down the front of the gown. These long seams draw the eye downward instead of across, as a natural waist seam break would do.

You can get all of these waistlines in combination with most all of the silhouettes, giving every bride a wide variety of gown choices.

It doesn't really matter which designer you choose. They will all have a wide selection of all of these silhouettes. When it comes to choice of designer, you may want to pay attention to their particular style, quality and customer service. When it comes to quality not all gowns are created equal.

Michel Bailey

Sleeves

Sleeves are a great tool for balancing. A great rule of thumb for sleeves is to remember wherever the sleeve ends, that's the part of the body the eye will be drawn to. (Herzog, 2013)

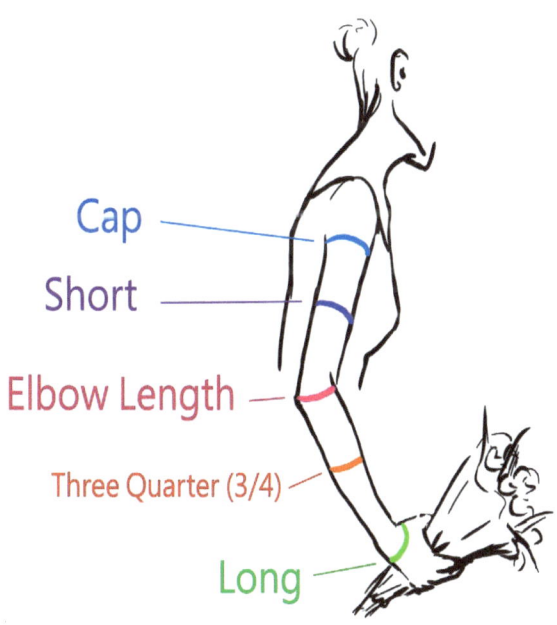

Sleeve Lengths

Here's the low down on sleeves:

A Three quarter length sleeve broadens the hips and makes the bust appear smaller.

Elbow length sleeves draw the eye to the waist, can break up a long torso and highlight the waist to show off curves also makes the bust appear smaller.

Long sleeves draw the eye to the fullest part of the hips.

Short sleeves draw attention to the bust and make the bust appear larger.

If you are big-busted, and feel the bust area needs to be minimized (in any gown silhouette), then wear a sleeveless gown or a three quarter or longer sleeve to avoid the short sleeve magnification.

The opposite is true if you are bottom-heavy. Short sleeves will help balance out the silhouette.

Here at Breathless Bridal we have sleeves that we sell with our gowns separately which can be sewn right into the dress. Because we are staffed by seamstresses, we often make sleeves for a custom look, sometimes using the extra fabric removed from the hem.

Sleeves are very popular at this writing, with the illusion base to work with, they are a lace lovers' dream!

Lace appliques, embroidery and beading can be sewn overtop the illusion sleeves to adorn any dress. Sleeves or straps can easily be added to strapless gowns to completely change the look. Many designers offer sleeved jackets called "pop-overs" that can be worn overtop a strapless gown. They come in a variety of embellishments.

Necklines

Another important feature of the bridal gown to keep in mind is the neckline. The neckline also plays a part in the balancing act between the bust and the hip/thigh area. (Herzog, 2013)

Here are the different necklines to consider when selecting a dress:

Narrow-Shallow: Narrows the shoulders and lengthens the torso. (Herzog, 2013)

Example: Shoulder edge ends in the middle of the shoulder area and has a neckline that crosses the collar bone or above. Some halters may fall into this category as well as Sabrina and square neckline if high enough.

Narrow –Deep: Narrows the shoulders and shortens the torso. (Herzog, 2013)

Example: shoulders edge sits in the middle of the shoulder with a V-neck or scoop neckline. Square, Sweetheart, Queen Anne and strapless could all have deep necklines.

Wide-Shallow: broadens the shoulders and lengthens the torso.

Example: wide set shoulders with a Sabrina or high neck neckline. (Herzog, 2013)

Wide-Deep: broadens the shoulders and shortens the torso.

Example: wide set straps on a V-neck or scooped neckline. (Herzog, 2013)

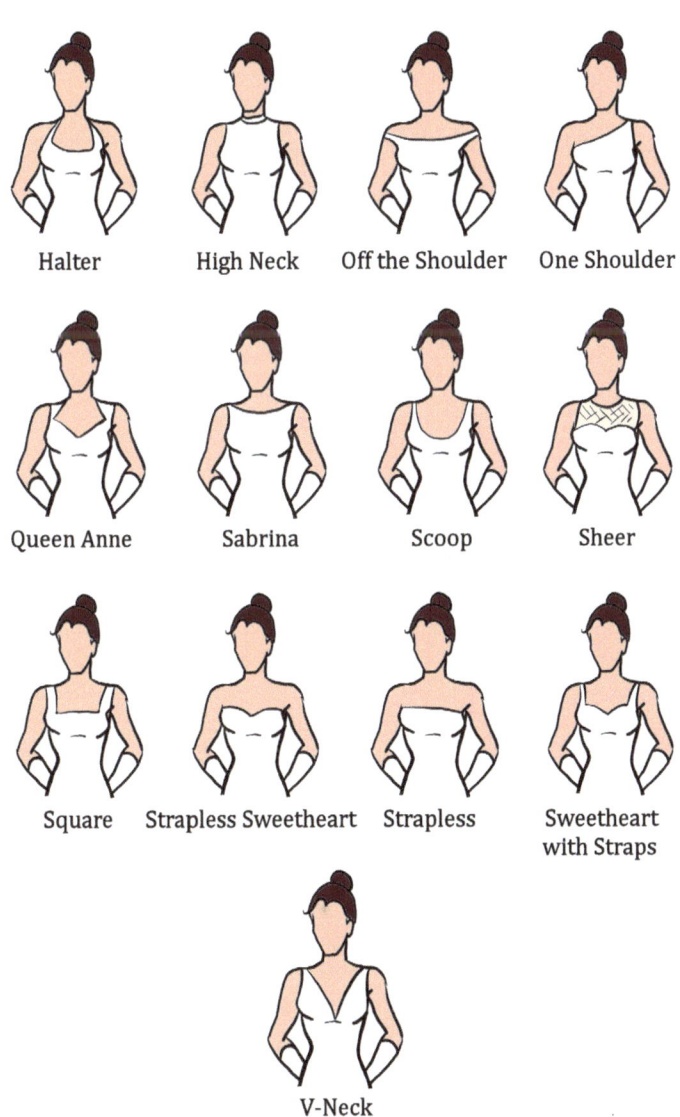

There are many options that can be added during alterations as well. For example, if you fall in love with a strapless gown, but feel your shoulders are too wide for this style to be complimentary, the illusion of the halter can also be created.

A spaghetti strap can be added to the strapless gown having them meet behind the neck. A strap can also be created from extra fabric from your hem if you want a wider strap.

Knowing the different effects the neckline can create, opens up a world of possibilities and broadens your selection of gown choices.

The Train

The train is the back of the dress hem that drags along the floor. Trains come in different lengths and decoration to create different statements with the gown. Here are the definitions of the most common trains.

Sweep: Sweep trains are very popular especially for a second wedding or a more minimalist bride. They extend 1 ½ ft. from the hem.

Court: Court trains are less than 1 ½ ft. long and begin at the waist, adding fullness to the entire skirt.

Panel: Panel trains are detachable and can be made to garnish any gown. They are fabric panels attached at the waist and can be any length.

Watteau: This train attaches at the shoulders and drapes down, giving a Grecian feel. A good alternative for a bride who doesn't want a veil, yet likes the look of a flowing veil.

Chapel: Extending 3 ½ to 4 ½ ft. from the waist, Chapel trains are one of the most popular choices.

Cathedral: Extending 6 ½ to 7 1/2 ft. from the waist. An exquisite train for a very grand day!

Monarch: Extends 12 ft. plus from the waist. The name says it all: it's a train fit for royalty or perhaps you? (WeddingsLDS.com)

All trains can be bustled with the same amount of ease, so don't worry about what to do with your train during the reception. The decision of the length of train should be based on the grand entrance and not easy movement after the ceremony.

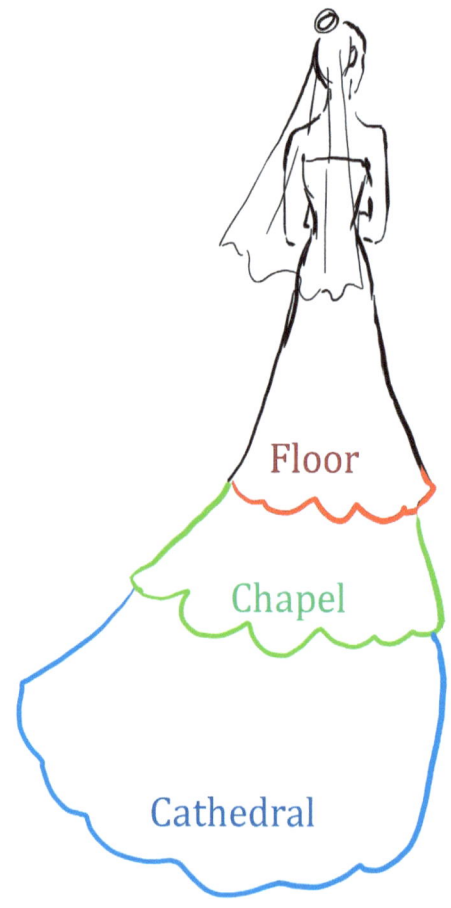

Designers

All professional designers will have a wide selection of the silhouettes mentioned here, as well as a choice of waistline and sleeve length combinations. When it comes to choice of designer, you may want to pay attention to their particular style, quality and customer service. Not all gowns are created equal! Well established reputable designers will have their gowns carried in brick and mortar stores. There are differences in quality even among designers found in bridal chains and boutiques. You can tell a good quality gown by its construction. Well-constructed gowns may have a bustier sewn into the dress. You will recognize this by what appears to be a wide bra strap in the back. There will also be plenty of boning sewn in the bodice of the gown to give it body.

Some designer lines offer plenty of customization options others just a few. Some of these options might include: adding sleeves or removing sleeves. Raising or lowering a neckline or changing the shape of the neckline all together. Depending on the designer, sometimes the gown can be ordered shorter or longer to better match the height of the bride.

***TIP:** There are not guarantees of quality when ordering from a website.*

I am all about customer service! I know I expect great customer service when I am a customer and I demand it from my vendors. When considering a designer, I want to know they will deliver what has been ordered, in the time frame expected. I also love a company that will go beyond the call of duty to fulfill an order. I will not mention names in the book, but your local store will know who they can count on! Again, only the best designers make and stay in brick and mortar stores.

Chapter 4

The Undergarments and Closures

Gowns are closed with either a corset lace-up or a zipper. Most dresses are designed with either one as the standard and the other can be a special alteration made to the gown at the factory when the gown is ordered; yet another advantage for ordering early!

Zippers are pretty straight forward and don't need to be explained. Most are concealed under decorative buttons to add an attractive look to the back of the gown. The dress will need to fit perfectly for a zipper to be utilized. If the dress is tight, there may need to be a hook and eye at the top of the zipper to prevent it from creeping down while being worn. Most zip dresses come with a hook an eye. If not, one can usually be added during alterations. If lost or damaged, hooks and eyes can easily be replaced. I'll give you tips on zipping in chapter eleven.

The corset back is one of my favorites because it is so forgiving. If the gown is too tight a corset can save the day! A corset is a lace-up back that can extend the opening of the back of a dress by six to eight inches. In our alterations department I have seen many dresses that were several sizes too small become not only wearable, but quite lovely with the insertion of a corset back. Again, gowns can be ordered most of the time with a corset and if not, one can be installed by a good bridal alterationist. Look for tips on the correct way of lacing a corset in Chapter eleven.

Michel Bailey

Crinoline

Our friend the crinoline! Crinoline is coarse netting that serves as an underskirt to increase the fullness and circumference of a gown. A few decades ago, crinoline had to be purchased separately and worn as a skirt under the dress. You can still order these skirt crinolines if your dress requires more volume. Designers today are sewing the crinoline right into the dress. Crinoline is not just for ball gowns anymore. You can find crinoline at the bottom of your fit and flare to bring the bottom skirt of the dress out. Most all gowns with any volume at all to the skirt will have a crinoline.

Bra Cups

Most dresses have a thin bra cup sewn in between the lining and outer fabric of the gown. Many times, an additional bra cup is needed to fill out the bodice area and to give the bust lift. A good bridal alterationist can sew them right into the dress so the bride doesn't have to bother with a strapless bra or other such garment. There are many sticky bras on the market to help cover if the dress is particularly silky and bra cups are not the best choice. Your local bridal alterationist can help you with these decisions.

Body Shapers

There are many body shapers on the market from waist shapers to full body shapers that extend to your thigh area. These garments are often made of elastic mesh and may help to smooth out unwanted bulges. This may be a good choice depending on the gown selected. Most gowns are made extremely well and heavy and often times provide the smoothing effect for you. Whether or not you want to wear a shaper will depend on the gown selected and how it looks on you. If you think you will want or need one, it might be a good idea to bring one with you to your bridal appointments. That will be the only way to know exactly how you will look in the silhouette you select.

Chapter 5

Fabrics

The silhouette is not the only important aspect to consider when selecting a gown. Fabric determines the feel of the gown, how it looks in sunlight or candle light as well as how it flows on the body. Many silhouettes can be purchased in several different types of fabrics which will yield an entirely different effect. Here are some definitions of the most popular fabrics being used in bridal gown construction today.

Laces

At this writing I think the lace gown is the most popular. We see mostly lace in our alterations department and we sell a lot of lace gowns in our boutique and no wonder! Lace is elegant and timeless! Gowns are made now completely of lace or garnished with a sprinkle of elegant lace to adorn the hem, sleeves and necklines. If lace is your choice, here are some facts to consider when selecting your gown.

Chantilly: Usually made of nylon, it's the most transparent of the laces. It is knitted like net and fragile. Chantilly lace can be found in fabric stores by the yard and can be used as a fabric to cover an entire skirt etc. It's usually placed overtop another fabric. (Justin Alexander Work Book South East Territory Spring/Summer, 2018)

Alencon lace or corded lace: can be made of nylon, polyester or cotton. It's a flat lace with an embroidered cord over it to give it a 3-dimension appearance. Point d'Alencon lace was created during the 16th century. It's nicknamed "The Queen of Lace" partly because it was Marie Antoinette's favorite. Many royal brides have worn Point d'Alencon lace during their wedding ceremony.(Alexander, 2018)

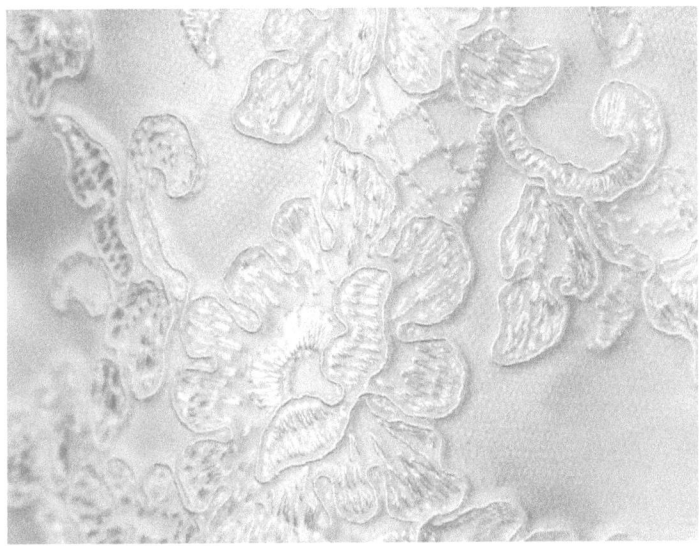

Venice: A thick 3D-looking lace which is made by heavily embroidering threads onto a dissolvable base. With the base removed, a heavier lace with a crochet-like feel remains. Can be made in cotton, nylon or polyester.(Alexander, 2018)

Embroidered: A thread pattern (which is machine embroidered) is sewn onto a tulle or base fabric, to create a lace like effect. (Alexander, 2018)

Fabrics

So many choices! Different fabrics do different things. Some give a light and airy look and feel while others stand at attention and give you that ball gown you've always dreamed of. A ball gown, for example, can be both a light and flowing gown or full and regal for a grand entrance. The difference is the fabric it is made from and the choice is truly yours!

Regal Satin: This is a satin with a shiny look and a softer feel, often found in alabaster and pearl colors. It is made of polyester.(Alexander, 2018)

Satin: Generally refers to a thicker satin with a stiffer feel and semi-shiny finish; made of polyester; often referred to as "bridal satin".(Alexander, 2018)

Michel Bailey

Chiffon: A soft fluid fabric, good for draping and Grecian style dresses and or Watteau trains. Chiffon is very popular for bridesmaid's gowns. (Alexander, 2018)

Silk Chiffon: Lighter in weight than the polyester chiffon. Silk Chiffon is very fragile which contributes to its fluid airy feel. (Alexander, 2018)

English Netting: Very popular at this writing. English netting is like tulle but has a heavier weight and a softer feel. It is stretchy, more fluid and very fragile.(Alexander, 2018)

Tulle: A netted fabric that comes in various finishes and weights. (Alexander, 2018)

Michel Bailey

Point D' Esprit: A fine bobbinet with scattered woven dots on tulle.(Alexander, 2018)

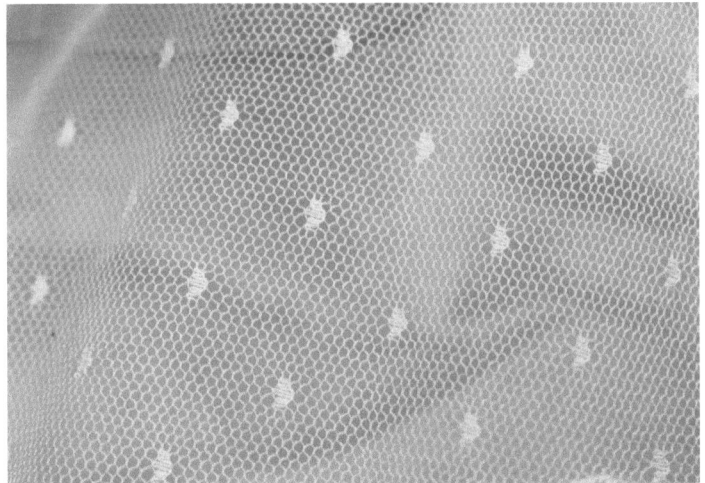

Organza: Semi-transparent woven fabrics with a matt or shiny finish which comes in different thicknesses to create different drapes or volume/made of polyester.(Alexander, 2018)

Charmeuse: Shiny satin weave fabric, with a soft fluid hand feel. Charmeuse is very popular in lingerie/polyester.(Alexander, 2018)

Luxe Charmeuse: Medium shiny satin weave fabric, with a much heavier weight and feel than normal Charmeuse, and considerably more expensive. Luxe Charmeuse is made of viscose/rayon.(Alexander, 2018)

Charmeuse is used mostly for inner linings today.

Dupioni: A matt finish fabric made of 100% silk. Dupioni is made from uneven threads to give its unique texture. (Alexander, 2018)

Weddings aren't always "white" anymore. The most popular color for gowns these days are Ivory or candle. Gowns come in many different shades and colors now. Blush is lovely and somewhat popular as well as gold or sand and taupe. Many of these choices have come about to compliment different skin tones. We recently had a bride whose wedding was in October and she wore black. A bride can truly have whatever her heart desires.

This gown is Pink champagne and Sand

Chapter 6

Where to Buy

Now that you have some idea of what gown will make you breathless on your wedding day, where will you find this treasure?

Well there are several places you can look and we will explore your options here and weigh the pros and cons of each choice.

Retail Store

The first choice that comes to mind is of course the Bridal Boutique or bridal retail store. Boutiques are fabulous because they offer all the latest styles, they should have a wide range of sample sizes and sometimes they have good sales or clearance for great deals.

As stated earlier, boutiques carry designer names, which offer excellent quality of gown construction. Construction is very important to how the gown will fit and drape over the body. Poor quality gowns can be spotted a mile away; examples might be ill fitted sleeves, no structure such as boning, and not enough seam allowance which can cause strained seams over tight fitting areas, just to name a few problems.

A good sales rep should be able to take your measurements to tell you exactly the size gown you need to order. They should have a wide variety of styles and fabric choices to choose from.

Most of the time a bride tries on samples and her gown is then ordered in her size and color choice. Here's the tricky part: if you have six months to a year before your wedding day, you should be just fine. It may take less time to get your gown in, depending on the number of gowns the company has in stock in their warehouse when you order. The delay comes when you have to wait for the gown to come from overseas in the next shipment. Your boutique should be able to tell you when you can expect your gown. Don't cut it too close because you WILL need alterations. Very few people fit the standard size charts. As stated before, gowns have to be ordered to fit the widest part of the body. So if you're a bit bottom heavy then the size gown ordered needs to accommodate that measurement. The bust area may be a bit too large. No problem! This can be taken care of during alterations, but you must have enough time to do it. So plan ahead! This same scenario applies if you are top heavy. In that case, the waist and hips may need a take in.

Gowns run long to accommodate tall girls wearing heels (5'9" usually), unless special ordering takes place; therefore most of the time your dress will need to be hemmed. Alteration time must be allowed in your timeframe.

With months required to get a gown in after ordering, it's always better to have a gown too long than too short. There simply may not be enough time to correct an order, which would require sending back the gown and receiving a new one. Depending on the company's availability, this could take another six months.

The greatest advantage of shopping at a salon or boutique is your wide range of choice. You have plenty of choices, IF you have plenty of time!

Many boutiques do have sales racks of last years' sample gowns. These dresses can be bought right off the rack so there's no need to worry about ordering, if you are getting married sooner rather than later. Choice is limited and you should check the gowns over for damage, spots etc. as these gowns are samples and have most likely been tried on many times.

Check the neckline for makeup or spray tan stains. Check the hem and train area for soiled edges or tears in the tulle or netting. Look for missing buttons, zippers that are broken or missing beads. Many of these things can be taken care of by a good alterationist.

On Line

Buying online seems like a great idea on the surface. Everyone buys online these days and there are great deals to be had. I become a nervous Nelly at the thought of buying a bridal gown online!

TOO MUCH RISK! Bridal gowns are a large investment and a once in a lifetime purchase! Not something I would take lightly or leave to chance. When you buy online from an unknown seller, you truly don't know what you're going to get until it arrives. This is a nightmare in the making! Most people consider this choice because they have a limited budget. I do understand that; however, there are plenty of great deals to be had in places where you can see, examine, and most importantly, try on the dress. I know, you have a friend who bought a wonderful gown at a fraction of the price online. She got lucky! I have seen many of these *wonderful* gowns in my alteration shop. The fabric is poor quality and drape of the gown is just sad and there is NO SEAM ALLOWANCE; which means you had better measure right, because if it's a bit snug there's nothing to let out. To sum it up: ***just don't buy online!***

Note: This applies to bridesmaid gowns also. Brides try to save their maids money by ordering bridesmaid gowns online. The biggest problem is measuring correctly because these on-line brides maid gowns **HAVE NO SEAM ALLOWANCE!** It is impossible to let the sides out and make them larger! This can be a nightmare for the bride and literally ruin the entire wedding. Remember you get what you pay for!

Secondhand

If you are truly looking for a bargain then consider buying secondhand. There are secondhand shops you can visit which usually accommodate trying on. Many of these gowns are on consignment. Sometimes the shop owner will take the initiative to fix missing buttons, beads, or a broken zipper. An honest shop owner will point these issues out to you. Nonetheless, look the gown over carefully so you know exactly what you are getting.

When buying secondhand, it's dangerous to buy a gown that is too tight. Secondhand gowns have most likely already been altered and may not have any seam allowance to let out. Only someone who knows how to check for this will know for sure.

On the other hand, the gown may have been taken in and there could be plenty of seam allowance. Hopefully the shop owner can tell you what the possibilities are for altering a particular dress. If you don't know for sure, **DON'T BUY A DRESS THAT IS TOO TIGHT!**

When buying secondhand, check the hem length. Keep in mind the heel height you wish to wear on your wedding day. If the dress is at the floor with no puddling in your bare feet, you will have to wear flats with that particular dress. Excess fabric is usually cut off of hems when altered, so there is no possibility of lengthening the hem. When it comes to hems, what you see is what you get.

Big name designer gowns are usually of excellent quality. Buying second hand isn't too bad if you are buying a good name gown. You can rest assured that the original construction is good. Your only concern will be: what was done to the dress by a previous alterationist? Is there damage from previous use? You must access the concern areas and make a decision if the gown is worth the additional monies for cleaning, in addition to alterations.

Remember, you are going to pay for alterations no matter where you buy, so factor that cost into your budget.

Another secondhand choice would be buying from an individual such as a friend or relative or perhaps off of social media sites. Again, I wouldn't buy a gown I didn't try on and examine. You may be able to get a bit more history on the gown, which may give you an idea of where the gown has been.

Ask where their venue was? Did they get married in a barn or outside? Did they have a beach wedding? This will give you some idea of what the dress has been through. If you know the person selling to you, you should have some idea of the care they may have taken with their gown. Just take your time when selecting your gown if buying second-hand. Remember deals that are too good to be true usually are!

Custom Made

Another option that seems to be rising in popularity is to have your gown custom made. This may be a fine idea if you are working with a big name designer who sketches a design just for you, as they do for Hollywood elites and the Royal Family. I think this sounds very exclusive and one of a kind to many brides who desire to be set apart from the norm, to me it just sounds risky unless Grandma is making it! What looks good in a photo or on a hanger can look completely different on the body. Can you be sure their sketch or photo will look as good on you?

Before trusting your most important garment purchase of a lifetime to someone with a great website, do your research! Talk to real human customers who have used this independent designer. Look at some of their previous work.

Usually this "custom" dress is made from a standard pattern that the designer uses. He or she most likely has several design patterns to choose from. Once the gown is made, guess what: you will need alterations. Why will you need alterations? Because of the standard pattern, it will have to been altered to fit your body shape. Hopefully he or she has included alterations in the initial price and will take care of this for you.

In my experience, I have had customers who have traveled great distances to have a gown custom made. In many instances the results are not that different from a gown purchased in a retail shop. Unless you want something very extravagant, custom made is rolling the dice. I'm not saying all custom made shops are not a good idea. I'm saying **BE CAREFUL**, know what will be included and check references (real human references.)

Never buy a custom made gown off the internet by sending in your measurements!

This is just a bad idea in so many ways! Measuring can be tricky. Send in the wrong measurements and you have a gown that doesn't fit. Again, you really don't know what you are getting until it arrives. If it turns out to be a bad deal, and I suspect that is what happens more times than not, you have wasted time and money. How will you rectify this situation?

You will have to put out even more money by buying a new dress or having whatever comes in the mail salvaged by a seamstress. There goes your savings!

Here's a thought: unless the designer designs a gown that only you will wear, then it isn't really unique for you, is it?

In conclusion, I think it might be important to ask yourself why you are leaning toward having a gown custom made. What is it exactly you are looking for in a gown or purchase experience? What can you settle for? What is a "must?" If you ask yourself a few soul-searching questions in the beginning and know what you truly want, it may just save you time, money, and heartache later on.

Chapter 7

Alterations

"You have to pay attention to alterations. I don't care how much you spend on a wedding dress. If you don't have great alterations, it will look cheap." Randy Fenoli, Rachel Ray show Youtube Feb 16, 2016

Definitions

Alterationist: Someone who takes a garment that is already made and alters or adjusts the seams to make it fit a particular person exactly or makes changes to it in some way, such as adding or removing sleeves.

Boning: It's called so because it used to be made out of bone. Boning is a thin, flexible piece of plastic sewn along the bodice seams, usually princess and side seams, to give the bodice stiffness. Boning prevents the fabric from relaxing and wrinkling as the body moves within the dress. Just twenty years ago brides had to wear a separate undergarment called a bustier in order to get the same effect that boning gives today.

Bustle: The bustle is created to lift the train off the floor so the bride can walk or dance freely after the ceremony is over. In spite of what you may have been told in the dress shop, gowns do not come with bustles! A bustle is unique to the brides' height. During alterations, it must be measured against the floor while the bride is wearing the gown, in order to get the bustle points just right. There are a variety of ways to create a bustle and usually the cut of the train and length dictate the most attractive way of bustling. A few examples are:

The American bustle: The train is brought up on top of the gown and usually buttoned up with a clear button. It usually takes three or four bustle points to bring the train completely off the floor. Very full gowns such as large ball gowns may take as many as ten or fifteen bustle points. The American bustle is the most common.

Ball Room Bustle: This bustle is created by bringing the train completely under and is usually tied underneath by coordinating ribbons that are usually color coded or numbered. When bustled in this manner, the hem appears the same length all the way around the dress; usually done on thick pleated satin dresses.

The French Bustle: The French Bustle is created by bringing the fabric from around the knee-point up and tying it on the underside of the gown. This creates a bubble of fabric. This is a very dramatic bustle because it is puffy, reminiscent of the bustles worn in the late 1800's. On the right type of gown, these bustles are very attractive.

Combination Bustles: These bustles are created by utilizing the American and French bustle techniques for unique looks.

Before You say "YES"

Dart: Darts are very short seams sometimes no more than two inches in length, usually sewn coming from the under arm area and pointing at the bust. These are called "bust darts." Darts create space for the bust in the bodice area. Darts can also be sewn at the skirt area to make the waist tighter as the skirt becomes fuller over the hips. If you have princess seams in your dress, you will not have bust darts.

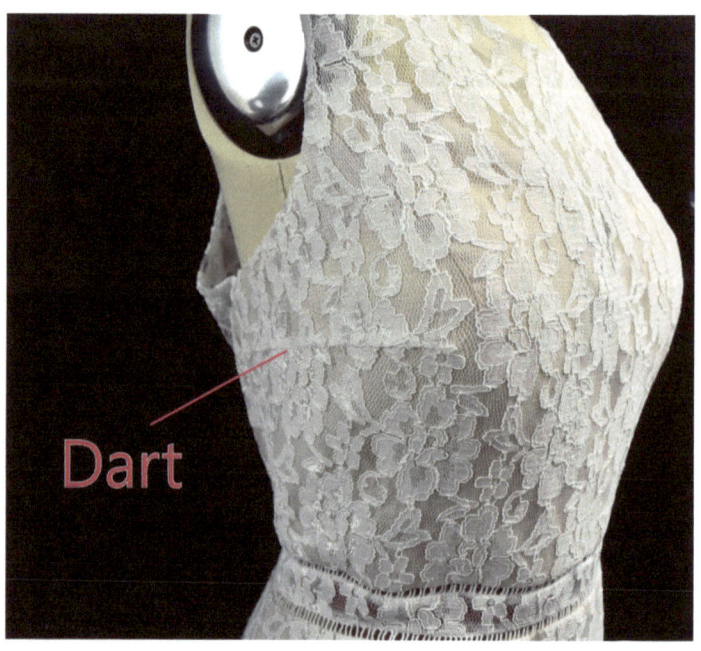

Hem: The hem is the finished edge at the bottom of the gown. To "hem" a dress is to make it shorter from the bottom. When pinning up the hem, every layer of the gown will have to be pinned separately.

Princess Seam: The princess seam is the seam that goes from the top of the neck over the bust. Depending on how the gown was constructed; this seam may run all the way to the hem. The princess seam can be taken in to make the bust smaller as well as to make a tighter fit in the waist and hip area.

Seamstress: A person who can sew and create garments. She may or may not do alterations. The term "tailor" is commonly used for seamstress however tailors most often deal with suits. For the purposes of this book, seamstress or alterationist will be used.

Side-take in: Increasing the depth of the side seam to make the dress tighter around the body.

Side-let out: Using the extra fabric at the seam or "seam allowance" to make the gown bigger when it fits too snugly.

Tuck: A tuck is a minor intake that eliminates extra fabric which may be puckering or bunching at any area of the gown.

What to Expect at a Fitting

As stated earlier, most every bride will need some sort of alterations if nothing more than a hem and bustle. The sooner you can get your dress in from the boutique and an appointment made for alterations, the better! Bridal alterations are not like normal alterations and shouldn't be trusted to just anyone. It is always a good idea to get someone who has a great reputation with bridal alterations and is familiar with working with the new designs.

Gown construction has changed considerably in the last twenty years. There is a lot more structure (boning) added to the dress as well as layers of tulle and delicate laces. Many gowns come with beautiful lace edges at the hem. Hemming a gown with details such as lace or beading takes expertise. All of these issues need to be dealt with and you want someone who knows what they are doing. What appears like a simple alteration to you, may actually be quite complex and, when done correctly, time consuming.

This is not the place to try to cut corners. Remember, you get what you pay for!

Depending on your area, alterations can book up month's in advance, so call early. Sewing and Alterations are a skill that is learned over time. It's not something you can just pick up in one quick class. Because of that, good alterationists are becoming scarce and bridal shops who have an alteration department are even more scarce!

It may be necessary to drive a good distance to reach someone you can feel confident in, again it's worth it!

When you will need to make your appointment is truly up to the alterationist. Because so many brides are dieting, scheduling can be tricky. Therefore, many alterationists don't want to have the fitting until four to six weeks from the wedding.

This is fine, but I know it makes some brides and moms nervous. You need to trust the alterationist. For people who'd call themselves "control freaks," turning over the dress and trusting it will be done on time is difficult, but that is exactly what they must do. Reputable alterationists in business have a system they follow. If they are not meeting deadlines or if they are turning out poor quality work, you'll know it! Great bridal alterationists have great references and reputations. Find a good one and then give him or her the time they need to do a quality job for you. Altering is a hand skill and unique to each bride, not something spit out by machine, that's why it takes time and patience on the bride's part.

In our shop, it isn't that the particular job takes a long time; it's that you have to wait your turn in line. We work off of the event date, so that we always have the gown finished in plenty of time. If you come for your fitting in April and your wedding isn't until October, doesn't it make sense that we would do the June wedding gowns first? Many people get anxious if their dress is waiting for a long time at the alteration shop, but unfortunately that's just the way it is.

Depending on the shop you are using, they may expect full payment up front. This is in case the wedding is called off and the bride doesn't come back. Your shop will give you their policies at the first meeting and if you have any questions, please ask!

A good alteration shop will be up front with their expectations and should give you a good idea of the schedule of events.

Bring all of the under garments you plan to wear with your gown to your fittings. Believe it or not, something as simple as a bra will change the way the bodice fits, even slightly. So you want your dress fitted just as it will be the day of the wedding.

It's very important to bring your shoes with you as well. If your hem is pinned in bare feet and you decide to wear heels later, the hem will be too short. **Shoes are one of the first decisions you need to make after selecting your dress.**

Depending on your gown, you may need to set aside a couple of hours out of your day for your fitting. I always tell my brides to plan on two hours. If your gown has a smaller skirt, one hour may be all it takes. It's probably a good idea to have the afternoon free in case the fitting takes longer than expected.

It's never a good idea to bring little children to a fitting. It can be a long, boring process for them and a bit nerve wracking for the bride and alterationist. It is also dangerous for the child if left to wander about. Fitting areas are full of dangerous items for children such as pins (perhaps on the floor) as well as scissors, seam rippers, and many other sharp objects.

A child allowed to jump off of fitting stages puts the child as well as the shop owner at risk. Plans need to be made in advance to keep children at home when going to a fitting.

Fittings can be a bit uncomfortable for the person being fitted as well. It's impossible to fit a person without using straight pins. Pins are placed in many different places during a fitting and many pins are placed horizontally in the bottom of the gown to hold up the excess fabric. I'm sure all aterationists take every precaution to make sure a "stick" doesn't happen, but a pin stick is usually not fatal and one should try to endure such a mishap with grace.

You may want to think about who you bring with you to your fittings. Fittings are very personal and the focus and conversation is all about the bride's body. Don't bring anyone along that you might feel uncomfortable knowing or discussing these topics in front of.

During that initial fitting, usually as many areas of concern are attended to as possible. Depending on the dress, it may take two fittings to address all of the issues. An example may be if the skirt is especially large, such as a ball gown. In the interest of not tiring out the bride, the bodice, hip, and hem may be pinned at one fitting and the bustle pinned at a later time.

A bustle with many points, may take a bit of time to get just right.

If the gown needs a lot of taking in, additional alterations may be necessary after the first sewing. The alterationist may not know this for sure until she sees how it looks after the first set of alterations. **Remember what you learned in physics: for every action there is an equal and opposite reaction.** That means, a large take-in of, say, two inches or more may cause a wrinkle or pucker to appear somewhere it wasn't before. No worries! This is quite common and the alterationist will usually know how to fix it. This is not a sign of lack of skill on her part, just what happens sometimes when things are adjusted.

A word of caution when standing for a fitting: it's very important NOT to lock your knees when standing.

Many brides have passed out during fittings due to locking their knees. Locking knees means standing very straight. It's always a good idea to shift your weight from foot to foot and bend your knees a little here and there. If you are concerned about the hem and afraid you will cause the seamstress to mess up, just ask her about shifting your weight. It's ok to take a break for a few minutes and walk around or sit for a minute.

We keep water and candy on hand for our brides during fittings just for this purpose. The alterationist can probably use a break as well.

For the modest bride, an alterationist can cover unwanted cleavage with a "modesty panel." Some gown designers sell modesty panels, so inquire at the boutique where you purchase your gown if one can be ordered to match. If the designer doesn't provide a modesty panel, the alterationist can sometimes use extra fabric from the hem to create a panel.

We offer free steaming at our shop if we do your alterations. You may want to ask if steaming is a service the alteration shop offers; even for a separate charge, or if you will have to make other arrangements. Steaming is a wonderful idea and almost necessary especially for exceptionally full gowns. During steaming, every layer is steamed separately and it "fluffs" the skirt to its fullest. It also eliminates wrinkles that were most likely caused during shipping.

Alterations are the one thing that make the dress truly your own. With a little knowledge and planning ahead it should get the gown ready for your big day.

Chapter 8

Destination and Themed Weddings

Destination Weddings

Destination weddings are all the rage right now and they certainly should be. Nothing is more romantic than a wedding on a beautiful beach in a tropical place at sunset. For this fantasy to take shape, you certainly need the perfect dress!

Many designers are now designing gowns with destinations in mind. So what should one consider when selecting a gown for a destination wedding?

The first thing to come to mind is the gown must travel well. The gown needs to be one that can take a plane to the fabulous location and come out fairly unscathed. The bride will have to decide if the dress will need to go into a suit case or can it travel separately?

We recently had a customer who purchased a dress for a destination wedding. Her gown was able to fly in the cockpit with the pilot! I'm not sure which airline that was, but it was very kind of them to accommodate her gown like that. You may want to ask the airline for suggestions and see what they can do.

Most likely, after a long trip the gown will need some freshening up. You will want to either find someone at your location to steam your gown or bring a steamer with you. How much steaming you will need, depends upon the fabric of your gown. Satin usually requires more steaming and wrinkles quickly. Chiffon also requires more steaming; however, it usually steams out quite quickly because it is so light and airy.

WORD OF CAUTION: *Be very careful about ironing your gown!* An iron can melt tulle and chiffon at the slightest touch! Both fabrics can be steamed easily, but ironing is another matter. When in doubt, **DON'T!**

Placing your gown or veil in the bathroom through a couple of hot showers will also help to relax the wrinkles.

Easy to travel gowns might include: A-lines, fit and flares, and straight gowns. Friendly traveling fabrics would include: chiffon, laces, English netting, and tulle.

Don't let the destination keep you from your dream gown! If you want a full ball gown, then that is exactly what you should have. Just bear in mind that arrangements may need to be made to get your gown there safely and back, as well as a good steaming after a long trip.

Michel Bailey

Themed Weddings

Themed weddings are just plain fun! This may include literary, fairy tale, vintage, and historical themes. For some of these subjects, a custom made gown may be in order.

Custom made may be the only way to get a gown that holds the spirit of the day.

If working with a professional seamstress or designer, be very clear about what you want the gown to look like. Bring pictures to your meeting to make sure they can fill your expectations. You could also go to your local craft store and peruse the sewing patterns for the style gown you want. You may have to check the costume section of the pattern book. If the seamstress isn't familiar with your style, providing the pattern will help the seamstress greatly.

I promised to tell you about my daughter's medieval/fantasy themed wedding. Her wedding falls under the category of "themed". Jesslyn, who is a fantasy writer and works with me here at Breathless Bridal, made her own medieval gown. She used a pattern from the costume section. She did her own sewing and I did the gold machine embroidery down the front. It turned out quite lovely.

My son-in-law wore a medieval tabard that he specially ordered from a costume magazine. The bridesmaids also had colorful fairy-like gowns that had to be custom made, which my mother and I made. The bride made flags that the bridesmaids carried and the nuptials were outside. It was a fun day and certainly a glimpse back in time.

Michel Bailey

Vintage weddings

Historically inspired weddings might include some lightly 1920's inspiration to a full civil war or revolutionary re-enactment ceremony. Many designers carry lightly vintage inspired gowns. The groom may or may not follow suit in his attire. Today's vintage gown may be a short dress with colorful heels.

Re-enactment gowns would be worn by the serious history enthusiast. These gowns are specially made with great attention being paid to how they are constructed as well as the finished look. True re-enactment gowns would be made entirely by hand with no machine seams. All buttons or adornments would have to be true to the period and either replicas or antique pieces.

Exotic Locations

Many weddings are taking place these days in exotic locations such as the local zoo, barns, islands, and boats! Your imagination is your limitation for locations, and there's a dress for every fantasy. Again, things to consider are where will you get dressed and enter, as well as how the dress will look in that location.

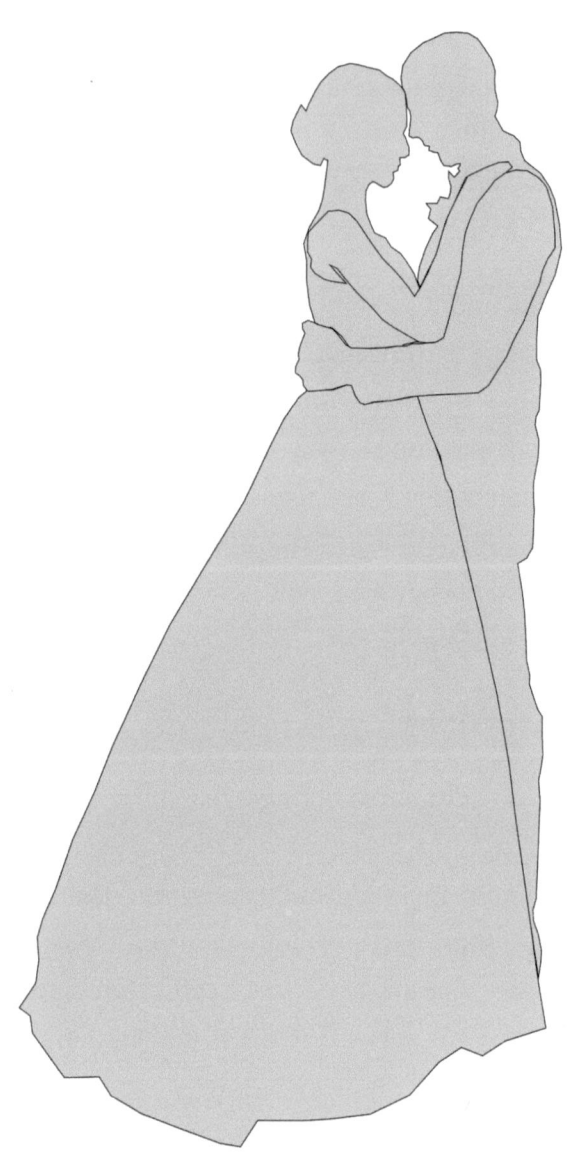

Chapter 9

Second Brides

With the divorce rate at fifty percent there is a large population of brides marrying for the second time. We see many of these brides in our shop and it is a pleasure to help them find the perfect dress. In decades past, there were so many social rules to second weddings. I think second brides sometimes still carry that weight around with them to this day, feeling as though certain gowns or styles are off limits to them, perhaps because they are over fifty or just because they have been married before.

I tell these lovely brides, "Have the wedding YOU want," especially to the divorced women. You are marrying the RIGHT man this time and why not have an ivory gown with a veil in the church if that is what you truly want? Why should the loser husband get the big shebang? When it's all over, you want no regrets. So have what you want! If other people in your life don't approve or like it: TOO BAD! They can do what they want the next time they get married.

Sometimes brides bring too many friends to their appointments and everyone has an opinion. I've seen brides who really love a dress, get talked into something they love less, because a best friend doesn't like it. Well your best friend isn't wearing it, you are! Be true to yourself. I think some of this could be because friends gravitate toward what looks good on them personally, not realizing that it may not complement you, the bride, as much. Brides need to buy the gown they love and that makes them feel beautiful, not the gown that pleases someone else.

Chapter 10

To Veil Or Not To Veil

After you have found your dream gown, what will you wear in your hair? There are many different things to choose from. Randy Fenoli says, "Without a veil, you're just a beautiful girl in a white dress." (Rachel Ray) The veil makes the bride!

Many brides these days are choosing not to wear a blusher, (the veil part that covers the face) and are choosing to place the veil on the back of their heads, most often in front of an up-do. Again there really aren't any wrong answers, only what makes you feel beautiful.

Veils come in an array of lengths and adornment, from lace edges to crystal beading.

There are very short veils which barely reach the shoulders, and cathedral veils which trail on top of the train and everything in between.

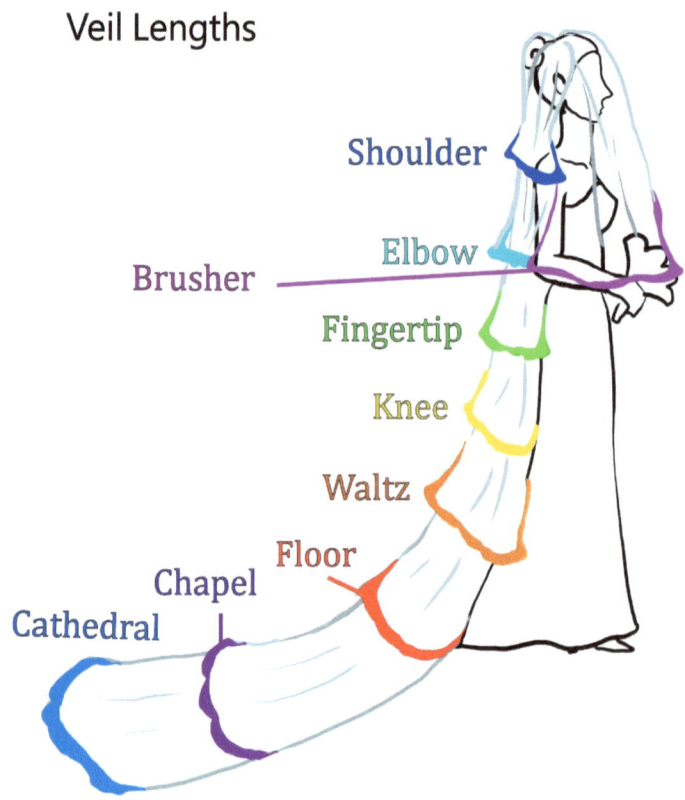

Beaded Edge Veil

Lace Edge Veil

It's a good idea to try on veils with your gown. This probably needs to be done at the time you purchase your gown unless you have the advantage of purchasing your veil where you are having your alterations done. Then you may be able to select a veil at a later time. You want to have your gown on when you select your veil. It's important to see how they will look together. A beautiful veil on the hanger may not compliment your gown the way you think.

Flowers are always an option. A sprig of fresh or artificial flowers in front of the veil comb may make a lovely combination. Combs with crystals and flowers may be a good choice for the brides who choose not to wear a veil. Veil companies usually offer a selection of beaded and crystal combs. Adorned combs are a popular choice for the older/second bride as well.

This is a perfect time to wear a tiara! Again there are many styles to choose from; thin bands of crystal beads and tall rhinestone adornments to name a few. The choice is up to you!

Michel Bailey

Chapter 11

Corsets, Buttons, and Bustles; "Oh My!"

The big day has finally arrived: the day you have been planning and dreaming of for what seems like forever.

Time to get dressed! Not always an easy undertaking. Let me walk you through some of the tricky parts.

Maid of honor and or Mother of the Bride, this chapter is for you!

Have the bride put her shoes on first. It will never be easier than it is right now, before the gown is on.

Next, step into the dress. This will prevent makeup from getting on the gown if you were to try to pull it over your head, not to mention what it will do to your hair!

Corset

A corseted back is the most forgiving of all back closures. If you have put on a couple of unexpected pounds, the corset will hide it well for you. However, lacing the corset is quite stressful for the one doing the lacing. Here are some things to remember.

Start lacing from the top of the loops and insert the ribbon **downward** to be sure the lace is lying flat on top of the loops.

Make sure the ribbon lies flat as you lace. The ribbon will take on the look of a rope if it begins to twist and you don't want that.

Next, cross the lacing, making an X, and insert the ribbon **up** through the loops.

Next, cross the ribbon and ***insert down*** into the loops.

Michel Bailey

Don't worry about pulling the corset tight until you are at least half way down the loops. When you do start pulling, **always pull the X's** that have formed on top. These ribbons (if made of a good satin fabric) are strong enough to take some pulling, so pull as tight as the bride wants.

Upon reaching the end of the corset, simply tie a large bow and stuff the ribbon, bow and all, into the bottom of the corset opening.

Congratulations, you've done it!

Zipping up

Zipping up is quite straight forward, but here are a few pointers. Getting the zipper past the seams can be challenging. This is common for a well-fitting dress. If one person can't seem to manage, you may need two people. Have one person hold the sides of the dress together as tightly as you can, while the other zips the zipper. Be careful not to catch a thread or fabric in the zipper. If this happens, try to move the zipper forward or backward until it runs passed the part where the fabric is hanging it up.

Once the zipper is up, and especially if the dress is tight, be sure to fasten the hook and eye located at the top of the zipper. A lot of dresses are coming with just a heavy thread for the eye part in order to disguise the hardware.

This may not be sufficient if the dress is tight. Have your alterationist change out the thread for a good strong metal eye. No one will see the hook and eye anyway when you consider how much will be going on in the back: veil, hair, buttons, etc. Tight zippers with no hook and eye may creep down which can be disastrous and stressful for the bride.

Buttons

Most zippers are covered with buttons and elastic loops. Buttoning these buttons give a finished look and hides the zipper. Again, this seems quite straight forward and it is. Simply button the buttons. However, these elastic loops can be quite tiny and it sometimes seems like your fingers get fatter by the minute. You may find it easier to start at the bottom and button up. If you have trouble with the buttons, and you should find this out during a fitting, get a crochet hook to assist in buttoning.

Before You say "YES"

Michel Bailey

Belts

Belts are a lovely addition to a gown and can add a dash of glitz and glamour to a simple gown. Sometimes it's the belt that brings it all together.

Many brides are opting to have the belt sewn right to the gown during alterations. This can be a good safe option as the placement will then be guaranteed and the ties can be cut off to eliminate the large bow in the back— if desired. If you want the bow eliminated, the edges are sewn down at the back seam near the zipper or corset edge. This method makes the gown appear to have come with the belt.

Some brides like the belt tied on and appreciate the bow in the back. It just depends on the gown, the belt, and the bride!

If you want your belt tied on, you should hold the belt in front where you want it on the gown, while someone ties it in the back. It will gravitate toward your natural waist. If you would rather have the belt placed higher on the body, such as for an empire waist, I recommend sewing the belt in place to avoid slippage.

Bustle

Nothing seems to strike fear in the heart of the mother of the bride quite like bustling the train! For good reason, especially if you have a large ball gown with fifteen bustle points. Have no fear; I'll walk you through it.

Your alterationist should tell you which type of bustle you have as well as demonstrate how to do it. When bustling an American bustle: start by bustling the inner most lining layer first, working your way to the outer layer of the gown. All layers will bustle the same. Start with the center bustle point on the center back seam of the train and then work side to side.

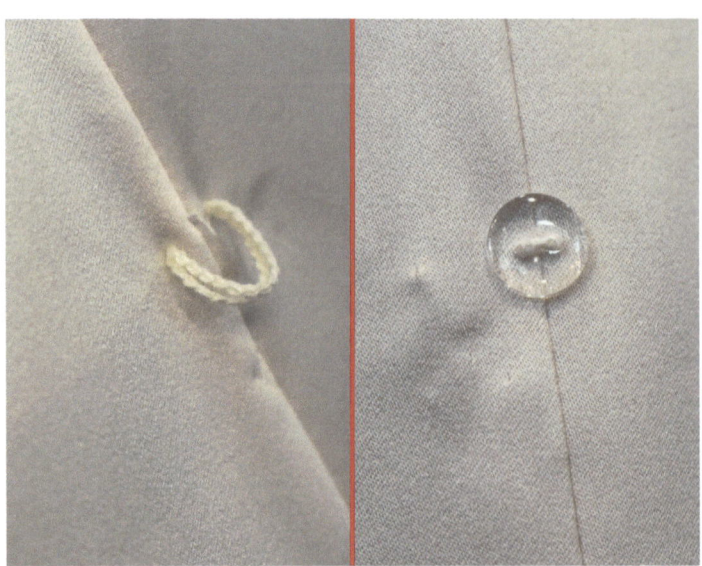

Run your hand up the center seam and you should feel a **knot** underneath. This knot tells you where your button loop is. Simply **pull up** on the thread and the loop should emerge.

The button that goes with this loop should be **directly above** the loop usually below the zipper or corset. Place the loop over the button.

Next, look for the loop to the side of the center seam. There should be another knot under the train that you can feel with your fingers. Again, **pull up** the loop and find the button that should be just above. Continue in this manner until the train is either off the floor or just brushing, depending on how the bride wanted her bustle to look.

Before You say "YES"

Now you simply fold the corners in to create a cascade of fabric. Bustles are gorgeous, especially if the center train has lace, appliques, and beading. Many designers have the bustle in mind when they design the train.

French Bustle

The French bustle is just as beautiful and gives an entirely different look to the back of the gown. The French bustle is created by bringing up part of the train and tying it up with ribbons. This creates a bubble of fabric at the back of the gown. The ribbons may be numbered or color coded, depending on the system the alterationist used. Again, she should go over all of this with you at your exit fitting. The French bustle's ties are usually attended to from left to right or vice versa.

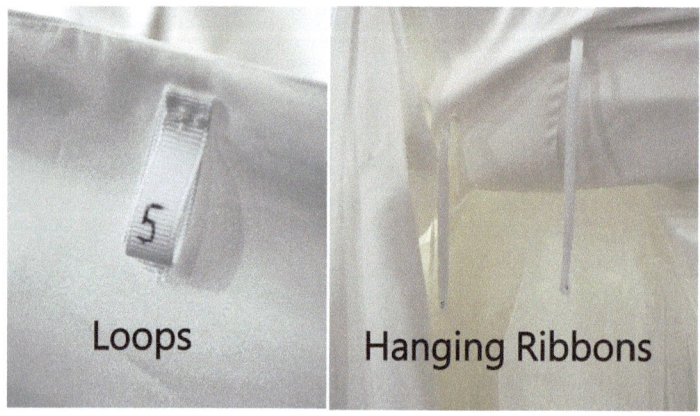

Loops   Hanging Ribbons

Michel Bailey

Combination Bustle

Combination bustles are created by combining the American bustle with the French bustle. In this case, you **start in the center** again which oftentimes is the American part of the bustle. Button as you would a regular American bustle. Then move to the sides of the train which is where you will probably find the ribbons for the French bustle. This could be reversed with the French part of the bustle at the center and the American points coming in at the side. Regardless, always begin at the center point.

The combination bustle may be necessary if the train has a rounded shape. In this example the Amercan point is in the middle and the two French points are on the side.

Michel Bailey

Ball Room Bustle

When creating the ball room bustle, the entire train is brought up so that the gown is floor length all the way around. Heavy fabrics, such as satin are perfect for a ball room bustle. Heavy fabrics don't drape well and an American or French bustle may not always be as attractive. All of this can and should be decided during the fitting appointment.

The Ball room bustle is tied up exactly as the French bustle. The difference is where the alterationist places the loops and ribbons.

Gown Before Bustling:

Before You say "YES"

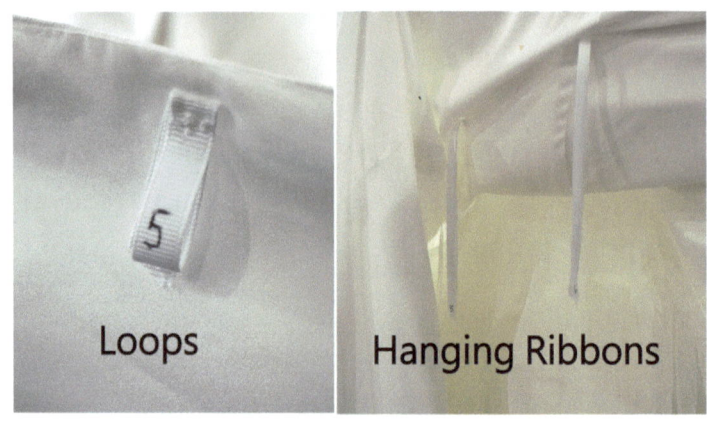

Loops   Hanging Ribbons

Gown After Bustling

Ball room bustles are easy because they are simply tied up with ribbon under the gown. Ribbons are usually color coded or numbered for easy bustling. Once again, attend each tie from left to right or vice versa. I do not recommend tying knots in the ribbon. At the end of the evening or when putting the gown away, this may be quite frustrating to take down. IF you are afraid the bow will slide out, I would tie the loops of the bow once again. This may take a few extra minutes to untie but shouldn't be impossible or as frustrating as a knot might be.

Start at the center back of the train and bring the train completely under and tie the ribbon found under the center seam of the train to the coordinating ribbon under the gown at the center back seam. If a very large gown, the bustler may have to put their entire head under the dress to find the ribbons.

Moving from side to side, continue tying until all ribbons have been used and the train is completely off the floor.

Attention Bride's Assistant:

You may want to have safety pins on hand in a variety of sizes just in case something gives way. If a bustle ribbon comes off, fold the end of the ribbon over.

This will give it strength and use as large a safety pin as needed to hold the ribbon in place. Safety pins can also be used on American bustle points if the thread loop breaks. Hold the bustle point up where it would normally be and try to safety pin it from the inside, so the pin doesn't show.

Conclusion

Shopping for the most expensive gown you'll probably ever buy; for the biggest day of your *life* can be a bit intimidating! Hopefully this book has helped you wade through the bridal noise and has given you a fun and exciting shopping experience.

As anxious as most all brides become when planning their wedding; try to remember at the end of that very special day, it's all about your love for each other and the new life you are starting together.

The little things that go wrong during wedding preparations or during the ceremony itself, need to be taken in stride and with a chuckle. It's the mishaps that make the memories!

Relax! Enjoy the process, and have a very long and happy life together!

Thank you so much for buying this book. It was a pleasure to write it. I have a passion for wedding gowns and the magic of the wedding planning experience. If you enjoyed this book, please consider leaving a review at your favorite retailer; and please come visit us at Breathless Bridal in Ridgetop Tennessee. We are always here to help you find your perfect gown!

All the Best!
Michel Bailey

Resources

Alexander, Justin; Justin Alexander Work Book South East Territory Spring/Summer, 2018

Fenoli, Randy; Rachel Ray show: Youtube 16, Feb, 2016.

Fisher, Lauren Alexis; How Meghan Markle's Wedding Dress Compared to Kate Middleton, www.harpersbazar.com ; Harpers' Bazar, 19, May, 2018.

Herzog, Amy, Knit to Flatter on line class at www.craftsy.com

Maloney, Maggie, (8 Suprising things you might not know about Kate Middleton's wedding dress www.townandcountry.com, Town and Country, 15,May, 2018.

https://wikipedia.org/wiki/wedding_dress_of_lady_Diana_Spencer

Diana Photo: Jayne Fincher/Princess Diana Archive/Getty Images
Megan MarklePhoto: Danny Lawson/AFP/GettyImages
Kate Middleton Photo: Kristy Wigglesworth/AFP/GettyImages
Shots by Cheyenne provided the front cover.
Find her on Facebook at: https://www.facebook.com/shotsbycheyennephotography/
Located in the Nashville area but will travel
615-310-7262

Veil Photo in Chapter 10 provided by:
Mandy Chadwick
Located in the Nashville area.
931-572-7536

About the Author

Michel Bailey has been a seamstress for 42 years. She has a bachelor's degree in psychology from Belmont University and a master's degree in Counseling Psychology from Trevecca University in Nashville Tennessee. She has four daughters and has planned 3 of their weddings--one more to go!

Michel owns and runs a thriving bridal shop called Breathless Bridal LLC in Ridgetop Tennessee, where they also include alterations in their services. She works with nervous brides on a daily basis to help them select gowns that complement their figures. During the alteration process she gives them a custom fit and transforms them into *breathless brides!*

www.ingramcontent.com/pod-product-compliance
Lightning Source LLC
Chambersburg PA
CBHW042334150426
43194CB00005B/156